D0065227

VOW

VOW

The Way of the Milagro

KAY LEIGH HAGAN

PHOTOGRAPHS BY RICHARD DOWNING

Council Oak Books
San Francisco / Tulsa

HOW TO MAKE A VOW

WHEN YOUR HEART IS OPEN,

BE IT AFLAME,

AFLOWER,

OR BROKEN,

WHEN YOU HAVE RECEIVED
A GIFT,

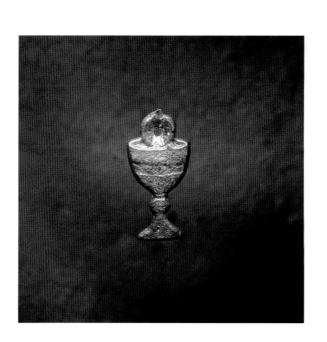

OR BEEN SPARED MISFORTUNE,

WHEN YOU NEED A
BLESSING,

OR A CURE,

To acknowledge grace,
before abandoning hope,

INVOKE THE DIVINE,
PRESENT IN ALL THINGS.

Ask for help,

ASK FOR HEALING,

SUCCESS, PROTECTION.

ASK FOR INSIGHT,

PEACE OF MIND,

OR MERCY.

In exchange,
make a promise.

DECLARE YOUR INTENT:

TO TAKE A JOURNEY,

TO DELIVER AN OFFERING,

TO BE A TOOL OF SPIRIT,

TO LIVE IN GRATITUDE,

TO REMEMBER, ALWAYS.

THIS IS YOUR VOW. NOW,
SURRENDER TO MYSTERY

AND FULFILL IT.

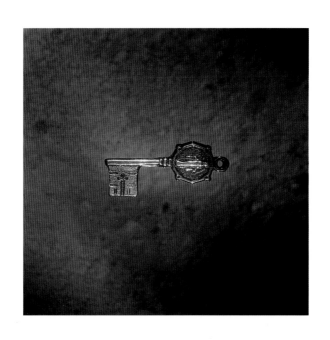

WHEN ALL IS SACRED,
EVERY ACT IS A DEVOTION.

Afterword

The images in this book are *milagros* or "miracles," miniature metal replicas of arms, legs, animals, tools, praying figures, or anything representing a concern or problem. Such charms are used as votive offerings to enlist the aid of the supernatural, or express thanks to the divine—deities, guiding spirits, and saints. In return for favors granted or blessings received, one makes a promise or vow: to go on a pilgrimage, to dance long and hard in ceremony, to repay the debt with devotion. This vow, *promesa,* or *manda,* is symbolized by the milagro, which is often worn for the duration of the vow's fulfillment and then offered at an altar, icon, or sacred destination.

Milagros in some form have been used for thousands of years in cultures around the world. Their use has been traced to the Aztec and Zapatec Indians. Votive offerings similar to the milagros used today have been found in archaeological sites from North Africa through the Middle East, across all of Europe, and as far north as Scandinavia. The use of such votive offerings is thought to predate recorded history in the Mediterranean. Today, milagros are much in evidence in the southwestern United States, especially northern New Mexico and Arizona, in Mexico, Brazil, and Greece. The milagros pictured in this book came from Mexico, Germany, Peru, Italy, and Bolivia.

Whether found in a Paleolithic-era cave in the Alps or in the candle-scented Santuario de Chimayó of present-day New Mexico, the milagro represents the universality of humans acknowledging the presence of spirit in everyday life.

Resources

Egan, Martha. *Milagros: Votive Offerings from the Americas.* Santa Fe, NM: Museum of New Mexico Press, 1991.

Oktavec, Eileen. *Answered Prayers: Miracles and Milagros Along the Border.* Tucson: University of Arizona Press, 1995.

Turner, Kay. *Beautiful Necessity: The Art and Meaning of Women's Altars.* New York: Thames & Hudson, 1999.

All of the milagros pictured in this book were found in the collections of these fine New Mexico stores: The Old Santa Fe Trail Gift Shop, Pachamama, and Doodlets in Santa Fe; and El Potrero Trading Post in Chimayó.

Kay Leigh Hagan is a writer, editor, and consultant, and the author of four books. She lives in Santa Fe, New Mexico.

Richard Downing's photographic sequences have been seen in short-form, documentary, and feature films, including *Common Threads, James and the Giant Peach,* and MTV shorts. His photographs have also appeared in books, exhibits, and periodicals. He lives in San Francisco.

Acknowledgments

My open-hearted thanks to Kevin Bentley, Richard Downing, Laura Jolly, Deborah Brink, Demétria Martinez, Elizabeth Wolf, Connie Hernandez, and Domenica Bianca.

Council Oak Books, LLC

1290 Chestnut Street, Ste. 2, San Francisco, CA 94109

1350 E. 15th Street, Tulsa, OK 74120

VOW: The Way of the Milagro. Text copyright ©2001 by Kay Leigh Hagan. Photographs copyright ©2001 by Richard Downing. All rights reserved.

Book and jacket design by Jaime Robles.

ISBN 1-57178- 097-1

First edition / First printing.

Printed in South Korea.

01   02   03   04   05   06   5   4   3   2   1